OXFORD UNIVERSITY POCKET DIARY

2023 – 2024

AF271458

OXFORD
UNIVERSITY PRESS

CONTENTS

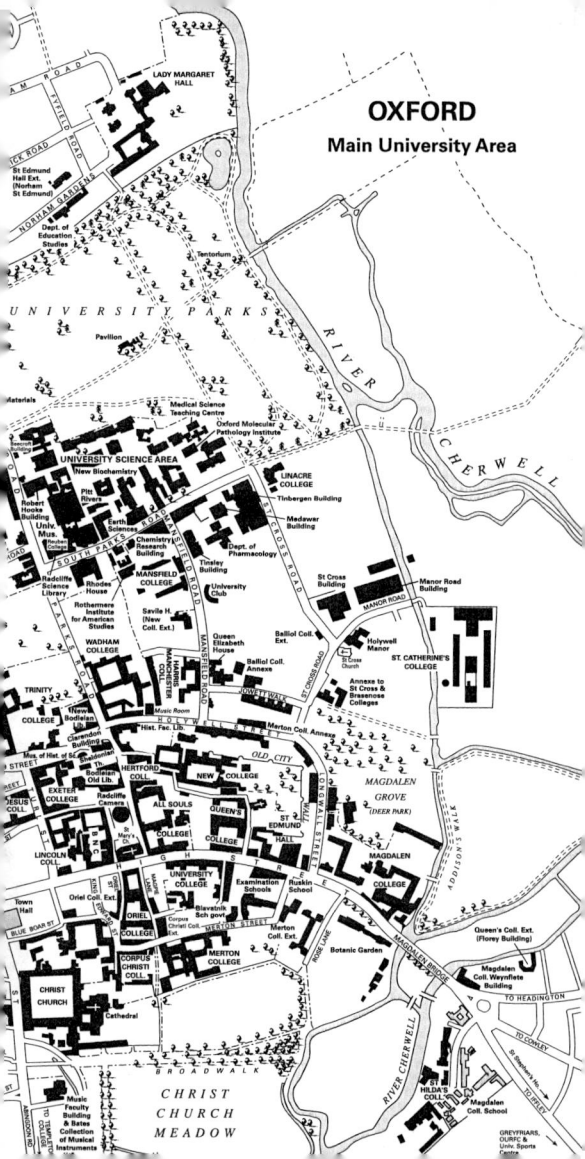

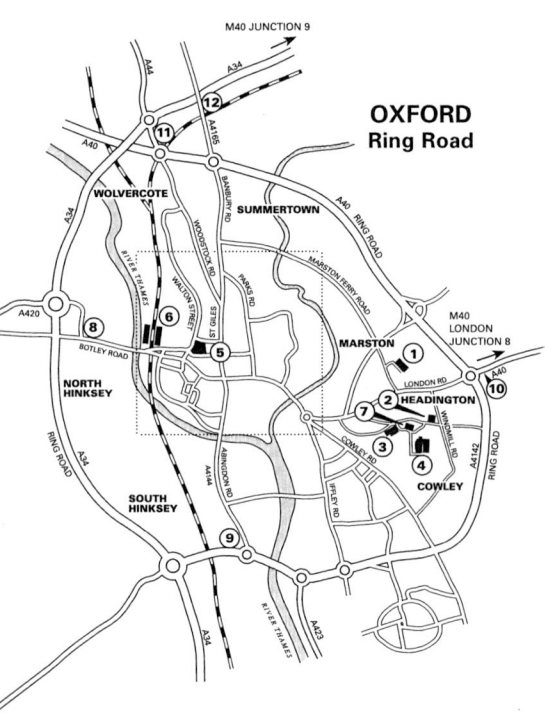

OXFORD
Ring Road

1. John Radcliffe Hospital
2. Nuffield Orthopaedic Centre
3. Warneford Hospital
4. Churchill Hospital
5. Bus Station
6. Railway Station
7. Old Road Campus
8. Seacourt Park & Ride
9. Redbridge Park & Ride
10. Thornhill Park & Ride
11. Pear Tree Park & Ride
12. Water Eaton Park & Ride & Oxford Parkway Station

FULL TERMS

2023–24
Michaelmas	8 Oct–2 Dec		
Hilary	14 Jan–9 Mar		
Trinity	21 Apr–15 Jun	ENCAENIA	19 Jun

2024–25[1]
Michaelmas	13 Oct–7 Dec		
Hilary	19 Jan–15 Mar		
Trinity	27 Apr–21 Jun	ENCAENIA	25 Jun

2025–26[1]
Michaelmas	12 Oct–6 Dec		
Hilary	18 Jan–14 Mar		
Trinity	26 Apr–20 Jun	ENCAENIA	24 Jun

[1]*Provisional dates*

DEGREE DAYS[2]

Michaelmas Term 2023
3, 4, and 11 Nov

Hilary Term 2024
20 Jan, 24 Feb, and 2 Mar

Trinity Term 2024
11 and 18 May

[2]*For details see: www.ox.ac.uk/students/graduation/ceremonies*

CALENDAR FOR 2023–2024

Figures in bold type denote days of Full Term

October 2023

Sun	1	**8**	**15**	**22**	**29**
Mon	2	**9**	**16**	**23**	**30**
Tue	3	**10**	**17**	**24**	**31**
Wed	4	**11**	**18**	**25**	
Thu	5	**12**	**19**	**26**	
Fri	6	**13**	**20**	**27**	
Sat	7	**14**	**21**	**28**	

November 2023

Sun		**5**	**12**	**19**	**26**
Mon		**6**	**13**	**20**	**27**
Tue		**7**	**14**	**21**	**28**
Wed	**1**	**8**	**15**	**22**	**29**
Thu	**2**	**9**	**16**	**23**	**30**
Fri	**3**	**10**	**17**	**24**	
Sat	**4**	**11**	**18**	**25**	

December 2023

Sun		3	10	17	24	31
Mon		4	11	18	25	
Tue		5	12	19	26	
Wed		6	13	20	27	
Thu		7	14	21	28	
Fri	**1**	8	15	22	29	
Sat	**2**	9	16	23	30	

January 2024

Sun		7	**14**	**21**	**28**
Mon	1	8	**15**	**22**	**29**
Tue	2	9	**16**	**23**	**30**
Wed	3	10	**17**	**24**	**31**
Thu	4	11	**18**	**25**	
Fri	5	12	**19**	**26**	
Sat	6	13	**20**	**27**	

February 2024

Sun		**4**	**11**	**18**	**25**
Mon		**5**	**12**	**19**	**26**
Tue		**6**	**13**	**20**	**27**
Wed		**7**	**14**	**21**	**28**
Thu	**1**	**8**	**15**	**22**	**29**
Fri	**2**	**9**	**16**	**23**	
Sat	**3**	**10**	**17**	**24**	

March 2024

Sun		**3**	10	17	24	31
Mon		**4**	11	18	25	
Tue		**5**	12	19	26	
Wed		**6**	13	20	27	
Thu		**7**	14	21	28	
Fri	**1**	**8**	15	22	29	
Sat	**2**	**9**	16	23	30	

April 2024

Sun		7	14	**21**	**28**
Mon	1	8	15	**22**	**29**
Tue	2	9	16	**23**	**30**
Wed	3	10	17	**24**	
Thu	4	11	18	**25**	
Fri	5	12	19	**26**	
Sat	6	13	20	**27**	

May 2024

Sun		**5**	**12**	**19**	**26**
Mon		**6**	**13**	**20**	**27**
Tue		**7**	**14**	**21**	**28**
Wed	**1**	**8**	**15**	**22**	**29**
Thu	**2**	**9**	**16**	**23**	**30**
Fri	**3**	**10**	**17**	**24**	**31**
Sat	**4**	**11**	**18**	**25**	

June 2024

Sun		**2**	**9**	16	23	30
Mon		**3**	**10**	17	24	
Tue		**4**	**11**	18	25	
Wed		**5**	**12**	19	26	
Thu		**6**	**13**	20	27	
Fri		**7**	**14**	21	28	
Sat	**1**	**8**	**15**	22	29	

July 2024

Sun		7	14	21	28
Mon	1	8	15	22	29
Tue	2	9	16	23	30
Wed	3	10	17	24	31
Thu	4	11	18	25	
Fri	5	12	19	26	
Sat	6	13	20	27	

August 2024

Sun		4	11	18	25
Mon		5	12	19	26
Tue		6	13	20	27
Wed		7	14	21	28
Thu	1	8	15	22	29
Fri	2	9	16	23	30
Sat	3	10	17	24	31

September 2024

Sun	1	8	15	22	29
Mon	2	9	16	23	30
Tue	3	10	17	24	
Wed	4	11	18	25	
Thu	5	12	19	26	
Fri	6	13	20	27	
Sat	7	14	21	28	

CALENDAR FOR 2024–2025

Figures in bold type denote days of Full Term

October 2024

Sun		6	**13**	**20**	**27**
Mon		7	**14**	**21**	**28**
Tue	1	8	**15**	**22**	**29**
Wed	2	9	**16**	**23**	**30**
Thu	3	10	**17**	**24**	**31**
Fri	4	11	**18**	**25**	
Sat	5	12	**19**	**26**	

November 2024

Sun		**3**	**10**	**17**	**24**
Mon		**4**	**11**	**18**	**25**
Tue		**5**	**12**	**19**	**26**
Wed		**6**	**13**	**20**	**27**
Thu		**7**	**14**	**21**	**28**
Fri	**1**	**8**	**15**	**22**	**29**
Sat	**2**	**9**	**16**	**23**	**30**

December 2024

Sun	**1**	8	15	22	29
Mon	**2**	9	16	23	30
Tue	**3**	10	17	24	31
Wed	**4**	11	18	25	
Thu	**5**	12	19	26	
Fri	**6**	13	20	27	
Sat	**7**	14	21	28	

January 2025

Sun		5	12	**19**	**26**
Mon		6	13	**20**	**27**
Tue		7	14	**21**	**28**
Wed	1	8	15	**22**	**29**
Thu	2	9	16	**23**	**30**
Fri	3	10	17	**24**	**31**
Sat	4	11	18	**25**	

February 2025

Sun		**2**	**9**	**16**	**23**
Mon		**3**	**10**	**17**	**24**
Tue		**4**	**11**	**18**	**25**
Wed		**5**	**12**	**19**	**26**
Thu		**6**	**13**	**20**	**27**
Fri		**7**	**14**	**21**	**28**
Sat	**1**	**8**	**15**	**22**	

March 2025

Sun		**2**	**9**	16	23	30
Mon		**3**	**10**	17	24	31
Tue		**4**	**11**	18	25	
Wed		**5**	**12**	19	26	
Thu		**6**	**13**	20	27	
Fri		**7**	**14**	21	28	
Sat	**1**	**8**	**15**	22	29	

April 2025

Sun		6	13	20	**27**
Mon		7	14	21	**28**
Tue	1	8	15	22	**29**
Wed	2	9	16	23	**30**
Thu	3	10	17	24	
Fri	4	11	18	25	
Sat	5	12	19	26	

May 2025

Sun		**4**	**11**	**18**	**25**
Mon		**5**	**12**	**19**	**26**
Tue		**6**	**13**	**20**	**27**
Wed		**7**	**14**	**21**	**28**
Thu	**1**	**8**	**15**	**22**	**29**
Fri	**2**	**9**	**16**	**23**	**30**
Sat	**3**	**10**	**17**	**24**	**31**

June 2025

Sun	**1**	**8**	**15**	22	29
Mon	**2**	**9**	**16**	23	30
Tue	**3**	**10**	**17**	24	
Wed	**4**	**11**	**18**	25	
Thu	**5**	**12**	**19**	26	
Fri	**6**	**13**	**20**	27	
Sat	**7**	**14**	**21**	28	

July 2025

Sun		6	13	20	27
Mon		7	14	21	28
Tue	1	8	15	22	29
Wed	2	9	16	23	30
Thu	3	10	17	24	31
Fri	4	11	18	25	
Sat	5	12	19	26	

August 2025

Sun		3	10	17	24	31
Mon		4	11	18	25	
Tue		5	12	19	26	
Wed		6	13	20	27	
Thu		7	14	21	28	
Fri	1	8	15	22	29	
Sat	2	9	16	23	30	

September 2025

Sun		7	14	21	28
Mon	1	8	15	22	29
Tue	2	9	16	23	30
Wed	3	10	17	24	
Thu	4	11	18	25	
Fri	5	12	19	26	
Sat	6	13	20	27	

Monday

Tuesday

Wednesday

Thursday

Friday

Saturday

LECTURE LIST   Hilary Term 2024

Monday

Tuesday

Wednesday

Thursday

Friday

Saturday

LECTURE LIST   Trinity Term 2024

Monday

Tuesday

Wednesday

Thursday

Friday

Saturday

MOVABLE FEASTS AND FASTS

	2023	2024	2025
Advent Sunday	3 December	1 December	30 November

	2024	2025	2026
Ash Wednesday	14 February	5 March	18 February
Palm Sunday	24 March	13 April	29 March
Good Friday	29 March	18 April	3 April
Easter Day	31 March	20 April	5 April
Rogation Sunday	5 May	25 May	10 May
Ascension Day	9 May	29 May	14 May
Whit Sunday	19 May	8 June	24 May
Trinity Sunday	26 May	15 June	31 May

OTHER RELIGIOUS DATES 2023/2024

Eastern Orthodox Easter	5 May 2024
First Day of Jewish New Year (5784)	16 September 2023
Yom Kippur	25 September 2023
First Day of Sukkot	30 September 2023
First Day of Chanukah	8 December 2023
First Day of Passover	23 April 2024
First Day of Shavuot	12 June 2024
First Day of Jewish New Year (5785)	3 October 2024
Yom Kippur	12 October 2024
First Day of Sukkot	17 October 2024
First Day of Chanukah	26 December 2024
First Day of Ramadan	12 March 2024
Eid ul Fitr	10 April 2024
Eid ul Adha	17 June 2024
Islamic New Year (1446)	7 July 2024

All Islamic dates are subject to the sighting of the new moon.

NATIONAL HOLIDAYS 2024

Austria 1, 6 January; 1 April; 1, 9, 20, 30 May;
15 August; 12, 26 October; 1 November;
8, 25, 26 December

Belgium 1 January; 31 March; 1 April; 1, 9, 19, 20 May;
21 July; 15 August; 1, 11 November; 25 December

Bulgaria 1 January; 3, 4 March; 1, 3, 4, 5, 6, 24 May;
6, 22, 23 September; 1 November;
24, 25, 26 December

Canada 1 January; 29 March; 1 April; 20 May; 1 July;
5 August; 2, 30 September; 14 October;
11 November; 25, 26 December

Croatia 1, 6, 7 January; 31 March; 1, 10 April;
1, 5, 6, 30 May; 17, 22 June; 5, 15 August;
3, 12 October; 1, 18 November; 25, 26 December

Cyprus 1, 6 January; 18, 25 March; 1 April; 1, 3, 6 May;
24 June; 15 August; 1, 28 October; 25, 26 December

Czech Republic 1 January; 29 March; 1 April; 1, 8 May; 5, 6 July;
28 September; 28 October; 17 November;
24, 25, 26 December

Denmark 1 January; 28, 29, 31 March; 1, 26 April;
1, 9, 19, 20 May; 5 June; 25, 26 December

Estonia 1 January; 24 February; 29, 31 March; 1, 19 May;
23, 24 June; 20 August; 24, 25, 26 December

Finland 1, 6 January; 29 March; 1 April; 1, 9 May;
21, 22 June; 2 November; 6, 24, 25, 26 December

France 1 January; 1 April; 1, 8, 9, 20 May; 14 July;
15 August; 1, 11 November; 25 December

Germany 1 January; 29 March; 1 April; 1, 9, 20 May;
3 October; 25, 26 December

Greece 1, 6 January; 18, 25 March; 1, 3, 6 May; 24 June;
15 August; 28 October; 25, 26 December

Hungary 1 January; 15, 29 March; 1 April; 1, 20 May;
20 August; 23 October; 1 November;
25, 26 December

Ireland (Rep. of) 1 January; 5 February; 17 March; 1 April;
6 May; 3 June; 5 August; 28 October;
25, 26 December

Italy 1, 6 January; 31 March; 1, 25 April; 1 May;
2 June; 15 August; 1 November;
8, 25, 26 December

National Holidays

Latvia
1 January; 29, 31 March; 1 April;
1, 4, 6, 12, 19 May; 23, 24 June; 18 November;
24, 25, 26, 31 December

Lithuania
1 January; 16 February; 11, 31 March; 1 April;
1, 5 May; 2, 24 June; 6 July; 15 August;
1, 2 November; 24, 25, 26 December

Luxembourg
1 January; 1 April; 1, 9, 20 May; 23 June;
15 August; 1 November; 25, 26 December

Malta
1 January; 10 February; 19, 29, 31 March;
1 May; 7, 29 June; 15 August; 8, 21 September;
8, 13, 25 December

Netherlands
1 January; 29, 31 March; 1, 27 April;
5, 9, 19, 20 May; 25, 26 December

Poland
1, 6 January; 31 March; 1 April; 1, 3, 19, 30 May;
15 August; 1, 11 November; 25, 26 December

Portugal
1 January; 29, 31 March; 25 April; 1, 30 May;
10 June; 15 August; 5 October; 1 November;
1, 8, 25 December

Romania
1, 2, 24 January; 1, 3, 5, 6 May; 1, 23, 24 June;
15 August; 30 November; 1, 25, 26 December

Slovakia
1, 6 January; 29 March; 1 April; 1, 8 May; 5 July;
29 August; 1, 15 September; 1, 17 November;
24, 25, 26 December

Slovenia
1, 2 January; 8 February; 31 March; 1, 27 April;
1, 2, 19 May; 25 June; 15 August; 31 October;
1 November; 25, 26 December

Spain
1, 6 January; 29 March; 1 May; 15 August;
12 October; 1 November; 6, 8, 9, 25 December

Sweden
1, 6 January; 29, 30, 31 March; 1 April;
1, 9, 18, 19 May; 6, 21, 22 June; 2 November;
24, 25, 26, 31 December

UK
1 January; 29 March; 1 April; 6, 27 May;
26 August; 25, 26 December

USA
1, 15 January; 19 February; 27 May; 19 June;
4 July; 2 September; 14 October;
11, 28 November; 25 December

*All dates are subject to revision. Half holidays and regional holidays are
not included.*

July/August 2023

30 Sunday   8 Sunday after Trinity
Sun rises 05.24, sets 20.58

31 Monday

1 Tuesday   *Lammas Day*
Full Moon 18.32

2 Wednesday

3 Thursday

4 Friday

5 Saturday

_____

_____

_____

_____

_____

_____

_____

August 2023

6 Sunday   9 Sunday after Trinity
Transfiguration
Sun rises 05.35, sets 20.46

7 Monday   *Name of Jesus*

8 Tuesday   Moon's Last Quarter 10.28

9 Wednesday

10 Thursday   *Laurence*

11 Friday

12 Saturday

August 2023

---

13 Sunday   10 Sunday after Trinity
Sun rises 05.46, sets 20.33

---

14 Monday

---

15 Tuesday   *Assumption of the BVM*

---

16 Wednesday   New Moon 09.38

---

17 Thursday

---

18 Friday

---

19 Saturday

_____

_____

_____

_____

_____

_____

_____

August 2023

20 Sunday   11 Sunday after Trinity
Sun rises 05.57, sets 20.19

21 Monday

22 Tuesday

23 Wednesday

24 Thursday   **St Bartholomew**
Moon's First Quarter 09.57

25 Friday

26 Saturday

August/September 2023

27 Sunday   12 Sunday after Trinity
Sun rises 06.09, sets 20.04

28 Monday   *Augustine, Bishop of Hippo*
Bank Holiday

29 Tuesday   *Beheading of St John the Baptist*

30 Wednesday

31 Thursday   Full Moon 01.36

1 Friday   *Giles*

2 Saturday

_____

_____

_____

_____

_____

_____

_____

September 2023

3 Sunday   13 Sunday after Trinity
Sun rises 06.20, sets 19.48

4 Monday   St Giles' Fair

5 Tuesday   St Giles' Fair

6 Wednesday   Moon's Last Quarter 22.21

7 Thursday   *Evurtius, Bishop of Orleans*

8 Friday   *Nativity of the BVM*
Accession of King Charles III, 2022

9 Saturday

_____

_____

_____

_____

_____

_____

_____

September 2023

10 Sunday   14 Sunday after Trinity
Sun rises 06.31, sets 19.32

11 Monday

12 Tuesday

13 Wednesday

14 Thursday   **Holy Cross Day**

15 Friday   New Moon 01.40

16 Saturday   **First Day of Jewish New Year (5784)**

September 2023

17 Sunday   15 Sunday after Trinity
Lambert
Sun rises 06.42, sets 19.16

18 Monday

19 Tuesday

20 Wednesday

21 Thursday   **St Matthew**

22 Friday   Moon's First Quarter 19.32

23 Saturday   Autumnal Equinox

September 2023

24 Sunday   16 Sunday after Trinity
Sun rises 06.54, sets 19.00

25 Monday   **Yom Kippur**

26 Tuesday   *Cyprian*

27 Wednesday   Ember Day

28 Thursday

29 Friday   **St Michael and All Angels**
Quarter Day
Ember Day
Full Moon 09.58

30 Saturday   *Jerome*
Ember Day
First Day of Sukkot

October 2023

1 Sunday   17 Sunday after Trinity
Remigius
MICHAELMAS TERM begins
Cambridge Michaelmas Term begins
Sun rises 07.05, sets 18.43

2 Monday

3 Tuesday   Cambridge Full Term begins

4 Wednesday   *Francis of Assisi*

5 Thursday   08.00 Holy Communion (Latin), St Mary's

6 Friday   *Faith*
Moon's Last Quarter 13.48

7 Saturday

8 Sunday   18 Sunday after Trinity
Sun rises 07.17, sets 18.27
FULL TERM begins

9 Monday   *Denys*

10 Tuesday   18.00 Court Sermon, Christ Church
Congregation

11 Wednesday

12 Thursday

13 Friday   *Translation of King Edward, Confessor*

14 Saturday   Matriculation Ceremony
New Moon 17.55

---

15 Sunday   19 Sunday after Trinity
10.30 University Sermon, St Mary's
Sun rises 07.29, sets 18.12

---

16 Monday

---

17 Tuesday   *Etheldreda*
Congregation

---

18 Wednesday   **St Luke**

---

19 Thursday   *Frideswide*

---

20 Friday

---

21 Saturday

October 2023

22 Sunday · 20 Sunday after Trinity
Sun rises 07.41, sets 17.57
Moon's First Quarter 03.29

23 Monday

24 Tuesday

25 Wednesday · *Crispin*

26 Thursday

27 Friday

28 Saturday · **St Simon and St Jude**
Full Moon 20.24
Partial Eclipse of the Sun begins 19.34, ends 20.54

October/November 2023

29 Sunday   21 Sunday after Trinity (or Last after Trinity)
11.00 Ramsden Sermon, St Peter's
Sun rises 06.53, sets 16.43
Summer Time ends 01.00

30 Monday

31 Tuesday   Congregation

1 Wednesday   **All Saints' Day**

2 Thursday   *All Souls' Day*

3 Friday   Conferment of Degrees

4 Saturday   Conferment of Degrees

November 2023

5 Sunday   22 Sunday after Trinity (4 before Advent)
10.30 University Sermon, St Mary's
Sun rises 07.06, sets 16.31
Moon's Last Quarter 08.37

6 Monday   *Leonard*

7 Tuesday

8 Wednesday

9 Thursday

10 Friday

11 Saturday   *Martin*
Conferment of Degrees

November 2023

12 Sunday   23 Sunday after Trinity (3 before Advent)
Remembrance Sunday
Sun rises 07.18, sets 16.19

13 Monday   *Britius*
New Moon 09.27

14 Tuesday   King Charles III born, 1948
Congregation

15 Wednesday   *Machutus*

16 Thursday   *Edmund, Archbishop*

17 Friday   *Hugh*

18 Saturday

November 2023

19 Sunday 24 Sunday after Trinity (2 before Advent)
Hilda
Sun rises 07.30, sets 16.10

20 Monday *Edmund, King and Martyr*
Moon's First Quarter 10.50

21 Tuesday

22 Wednesday *Cecilia*

23 Thursday *Clement*

24 Friday

25 Saturday *Catherine*

November/December 2023

26 Sunday   Sunday next before Advent (Christ the King)
18.00 University Sermon (on the Sin of Pride), Keble
Sun rises 07.42, sets 16.02

27 Monday   Full Moon 09.16

28 Tuesday   Congregation

29 Wednesday

30 Thursday   **St Andrew**
Matriculation Ceremony

1 Friday   Cambridge Full Term ends

2 Saturday   **FULL TERM ends**

December 2023

---

3 Sunday   1 Sunday in Advent
11.00 University Sermon (Advent), Christ Church
Sun rises 07.52, sets 15.57

---

4 Monday

---

5 Tuesday   Moon's Last Quarter 05.49

---

6 Wednesday   *Nicolas*

---

7 Thursday

---

8 Friday   *Conception of the BVM*
First Day of Chanukah

---

9 Saturday

December 2023

10 Sunday   2 Sunday in Advent
Sun rises 08.00, sets 15.55

11 Monday

12 Tuesday   Congregation
New Moon 23.32

13 Wednesday   *Lucy*
Ember Day

14 Thursday

15 Friday   Ember Day

16 Saturday   *O Sapientia*
Ember Day

December 2023

17 Sunday   3 Sunday in Advent
MICHAELMAS TERM ends
Sun rises 08.07, sets 15.55

18 Monday

19 Tuesday   Cambridge Michaelmas Term ends
Moon's First Quarter 18.39

20 Wednesday

21 Thursday   **St Thomas**

22 Friday   Winter Solstice

23 Saturday

December 2023

24 Sunday   4 Sunday in Advent
Sun rises 08.11, sets 15.58

25 Monday   **Christmas Day**
Quarter Day
Bank Holiday

26 Tuesday   **St Stephen**
Bank Holiday

27 Wednesday   **St John the Evangelist**
Full Moon 00.33

28 Thursday   **Innocents' Day**

29 Friday

30 Saturday

_____

_____

_____

_____

_____

_____

_____

31 Sunday   1 Sunday after Christmas
Silvester
Sun rises 08.12, sets 16.04

1 Monday   **Circumcision (Naming of Jesus)**
Bank Holiday

2 Tuesday

3 Wednesday

4 Thursday   Moon's Last Quarter 03.30

5 Friday   Cambridge Lent Term begins

6 Saturday   **The Epiphany**

January 2024

7 Sunday   1 Sunday after Epiphany (Baptism of Christ)
HILARY TERM begins
Sun rises 08.11, sets 16.12

8 Monday   *Lucian*

9 Tuesday

10 Wednesday

11 Thursday   08.00 Holy Communion (Latin), St Mary's
New Moon 11.57

12 Friday

13 Saturday   *Hilary*

January 2024

14 Sunday 2 Sunday after Epiphany
15.30 Latin Litany and Sermon, St Mary's
Sun rises 08.06, sets 16.22
FULL TERM begins

15 Monday

16 Tuesday Cambridge Full Term begins
Congregation

17 Wednesday *Antony*

18 Thursday *Prisca*
Moon's First Quarter 03.53

19 Friday

20 Saturday *Fabian*
Conferment of Degrees

January 2024

---

21 Sunday   3 Sunday after Epiphany
Agnes
10.00 Macbride Sermon, Hertford College
Sun rises 08.00, sets 16.33

---

22 Monday   *Vincent*

---

23 Tuesday   Congregation

---

24 Wednesday

---

25 Thursday   **Conversion of St Paul**
Full Moon 17.54

---

26 Friday

---

27 Saturday

28 Sunday   Septuagesima (4 Sunday after Epiphany)
Sun rises 07.51, sets 16.45

29 Monday

30 Tuesday   *Charles I, King and Martyr*

31 Wednesday

1 Thursday

2 Friday   **Presentation of Christ in the Temple**
Candlemas Day
Moon's Last Quarter 23.18

3 Saturday   *Blasius*

February 2024

4 Sunday   Sexagesima (2 Sunday before Lent)
17.30 University Sermon and Inter-Collegiate
Evensong, St Mary's
Sun rises 07.40, sets 16.58

5 Monday   *Agatha*

6 Tuesday   Congregation

7 Wednesday

8 Thursday

9 Friday   New Moon 22.59

10 Saturday   *Scholastica*
Festum Ovorum

February 2024

11 Sunday   Quinquagesima (Sunday next before Lent)
17.45 University Sermon (on the Grace of Humility),
Lady Margaret Hall
Sun rises 07.28, sets 17.11

12 Monday

13 Tuesday   Shrove Tuesday

14 Wednesday   **Ash Wednesday**
Valentine

15 Thursday

16 Friday   Moon's First Quarter 15.01

17 Saturday

February 2024

---

18 Sunday   1 Sunday in Lent
Sun rises 07.15, sets 17.24

---

19 Monday

---

20 Tuesday   Congregation

---

21 Wednesday   Ember Day

---

22 Thursday

---

23 Friday   Ember Day

---

24 Saturday   **St Matthias**
Ember Day
Conferment of Degrees
Full Moon 12.30

25 Sunday   2 Sunday in Lent
10.30 University Sermon, St Mary's
Sun rises 07.00, sets 17.37

26 Monday

27 Tuesday

28 Wednesday   Torpids

29 Thursday   Torpids

1 Friday   *David*
Torpids

2 Saturday   *Chad*
Torpids
Conferment of Degrees

March 2024

3 Sunday
3 Sunday in Lent
18.00 Sermon for the Annunciation of the Blessed
Virgin Mary, Oriel College
Sun rises 06.45, sets 17.49
Moon's Last Quarter 15.23

4 Monday

5 Tuesday   Congregation

6 Wednesday   Election of Proctors and Assessor for 2025–26

7 Thursday   *Perpetua*
Matriculation Ceremony

8 Friday

9 Saturday   **FULL TERM ends**

March 2024

10 Sunday   4 Sunday in Lent
Mothering Sunday
Sun rises 06.30, sets 18.02
New Moon 09.00

11 Monday   Commonwealth Day

12 Tuesday   *Gregory*
First Day of Ramadan

13 Wednesday   Admission of Proctors and Assessor for 2024–25

14 Thursday

15 Friday   Cambridge Full Term ends

16 Saturday

---

17 Sunday   5 Sunday in Lent
Patrick
Sun rises 06.14, sets 18.14
Moon's First Quarter 04.11

---

18 Monday   *Edward, King of the West Saxons*

---

19 Tuesday   **St Joseph**
Congregation

---

20 Wednesday   *Cuthbert*
Vernal Equinox

---

21 Thursday   *Benedict*

---

22 Friday

---

23 Saturday   **HILARY TERM ends**

March 2024

24 Sunday   Sunday next before Easter (Palm Sunday)
Cambridge Lent Term ends
Sun rises 05.58, sets 18.26

25 Monday   Quarter Day
Full Moon 07.00

26 Tuesday

27 Wednesday

28 Thursday   **Maundy Thursday**

29 Friday   **Good Friday**
Bank Holiday

30 Saturday   **Easter Eve**
Boat Race

_____

_____

_____

_____

_____

_____

_____

March/April 2024

31 Sunday   **Easter Day**
Sun rises 06.41, sets 19.38
Summer Time begins 01.00

1 Monday   Bank Holiday

2 Tuesday   Moon's Last Quarter 03.15

3 Wednesday   *Richard, Bishop of Chichester*

4 Thursday   *Ambrose*

5 Friday

6 Saturday

April 2024

7 Sunday   1 Sunday after Easter (2 of Easter)
Low Sunday
Sun rises 06.26, sets 19.49

8 Monday   **Annunciation of the BVM**
New Moon 18.21

9 Tuesday

10 Wednesday   **Eid ul Fitr**

11 Thursday

12 Friday

13 Saturday

_____

_____

_____

_____

_____

_____

_____

April 2024

14 Sunday   2 Sunday after Easter (3 of Easter)
Sun rises 06.10, sets 20.01

15 Monday   Moon's First Quarter 19.13

16 Tuesday

17 Wednesday   Cambridge Easter Term begins

18 Thursday   08.00 Holy Communion (Latin), St Mary's

19 Friday   *Alphege*

20 Saturday   **TRINITY TERM begins**

April 2024

21 Sunday   3 Sunday after Easter (4 of Easter)
18.00 St Mark's Day Sermon, Magdalen College
FULL TERM begins
Sun rises 05.55, sets 20.13

22 Monday

23 Tuesday   **St George**
First Day of Passover
Cambridge Full Term begins
Congregation
Full Moon 23.49

24 Wednesday

25 Thursday   **St Mark**

26 Friday

27 Saturday

April/May 2024

28 Sunday   4 Sunday after Easter (5 of Easter)
Sun rises 05.41, sets 20.25

29 Monday

30 Tuesday   Congregation

1 Wednesday   **St Philip and St James**
Moon's Last Quarter 11.27

2 Thursday

3 Friday   *Invention of the Cross*

4 Saturday

May 2024

---

5 Sunday   5 Sunday after Easter (6 of Easter)
Rogation Sunday
Eastern Orthodox Easter
10.30 University Commemoration Day Sermon,
St Mary's
Sun rises 05.28, sets 20.36

---

6 Monday   *St John ante Portam Latinam*
Rogation Day
Bank Holiday
Coronation of King Charles III, 2023

---

7 Tuesday   Rogation Day

---

8 Wednesday   Rogation Day
New Moon 03.22

---

9 Thursday   **Ascension Day**

---

10 Friday

---

11 Saturday   Conferment of Degrees

May 2024

---

12 Sunday   Sunday after Ascension Day (7 of Easter)
10.30 University Sermon, St Mary's
Sun rises 05.16, sets 20.48

---

13 Monday

---

14 Tuesday   **(St Matthias)**
Congregation

---

15 Wednesday   Moon's First Quarter 11.48

---

16 Thursday

---

17 Friday

---

18 Saturday   Conferment of Degrees

May 2024

19 Sunday   **Whit Sunday (Pentecost)**
Dunstan
09.45 University Sermon, Christ Church
Sun rises 05.06, sets 20.58

20 Monday

21 Tuesday

22 Wednesday   Eights

23 Thursday   Eights
Full Moon 13.53

24 Friday   *John and Charles Wesley*
Eights

25 Saturday   Eights

May/June 2024

---

26 Sunday   **Trinity Sunday**
Augustine, Archbishop of Canterbury
18.15 University Sermon, The Queen's College
Sun rises 04.57, sets 21.08

---

27 Monday   *Bede*
Bank Holiday

---

28 Tuesday   Congregation

---

29 Wednesday

---

30 Thursday   *Corpus Christi*
Moon's Last Quarter 17.13

---

31 Friday   **(Visit of the BVM to Elizabeth)**

---

1 Saturday   *Nicomede*

June 2024

2 Sunday   1 Sunday after Trinity
Sun rises 04.51, sets 21.16

3 Monday

4 Tuesday

5 Wednesday   *Boniface*

6 Thursday   New Moon 12.38

7 Friday

8 Saturday   King's Official Birthday (provisional date)

June 2024

9 Sunday   2 Sunday after Trinity
Columba
Sun rises 04.47, sets 21.22

10 Monday

11 Tuesday   **St Barnabas**
Congregation

12 Wednesday   **First Day of Shavuot**

13 Thursday   Matriculation Ceremony

14 Friday   Cambridge Full Term ends
Moon's First Quarter 05.18

15 Saturday   **FULL TERM ends**

June 2024

16 Sunday   3 Sunday after Trinity
10.00 St John Baptist's Day Sermon, Magdalen College
Sun rises 04.46, sets 21.26

17 Monday   **Eid ul Adha**

18 Tuesday

19 Wednesday   Encaenia

20 Thursday   *Translation of Edward, King of the West Saxons*
Summer Solstice

21 Friday   Prince of Wales born, 1982

22 Saturday   *Alban*
Full Moon 01.08

June 2024

---

23 Sunday   4 Sunday after Trinity
Sun rises 04.47, sets 21.28

---

24 Monday   **Nativity of St John the Baptist**
Quarter Day

---

25 Tuesday   Congregation
Cambridge Easter Term ends

---

26 Wednesday   Ember Day

---

27 Thursday

---

28 Friday   Ember Day
Moon's Last Quarter 21.53

---

29 Saturday   **St Peter**
Ember Day

30 Sunday   5 Sunday after Trinity
Sun rises 04.50, sets 21.27

1 Monday

2 Tuesday   *Visitation of the BVM*

3 Wednesday   **(St Thomas)**

4 Thursday   *Translation of St Martin*

5 Friday   New Moon 22.57

6 Saturday   **TRINITY TERM ends**

July 2024

7 Sunday   6 Sunday after Trinity
Islamic New Year (1446)
Sun rises 04.56, sets 21.24

8 Monday

9 Tuesday

10 Wednesday

11 Thursday

12 Friday

13 Saturday   Moon's First Quarter 22.49

July 2024

14 Sunday   7 Sunday after Trinity
John Keble
Sun rises 05.03, sets 21.18

15 Monday   *Swithun*

16 Tuesday

17 Wednesday   Queen Camilla born, 1947

18 Thursday

19 Friday

20 Saturday   *Margaret*

_____

_____

_____

_____

_____

_____

_____

July 2024

21 Sunday   8 Sunday after Trinity
Sun rises 05.12, sets 21.10
Full Moon 10.17

22 Monday   **St Mary Magdalen**

23 Tuesday

24 Wednesday

25 Thursday   **St James**

26 Friday   *Anne*

27 Saturday

28 Sunday   9 Sunday after Trinity
Sun rises 05.22, sets 21.00
Moon's Last Quarter 02.52

29 Monday

30 Tuesday

31 Wednesday

1 Thursday   *Lammas Day*

2 Friday

3 Saturday

August 2024

4 Sunday   10 Sunday after Trinity
Sun rises 05.33, sets 20.48
New Moon 11.13

5 Monday

6 Tuesday   **Transfiguration**

7 Wednesday   *Name of Jesus*

8 Thursday

9 Friday

10 Saturday   *Laurence*

_____

_____

_____

_____

_____

_____

_____

August 2024

11 Sunday   11 Sunday after Trinity
Sun rises 05.44, sets 20.35

12 Monday   Moon's First Quarter 15.19

13 Tuesday

14 Wednesday

15 Thursday   *Assumption of the BVM*

16 Friday

17 Saturday

18 Sunday   12 Sunday after Trinity
Sun rises 05.55, sets 20.21

19 Monday   Full Moon 18.26

20 Tuesday

21 Wednesday

22 Thursday

23 Friday

24 Saturday   **St Bartholomew**

August 2024

25 Sunday   13 Sunday after Trinity
Sun rises 06.06, sets 20.06

26 Monday   Bank Holiday
Moon's Last Quarter 09.26

27 Tuesday

28 Wednesday   *Augustine, Bishop of Hippo*

29 Thursday   *Beheading of St John the Baptist*

30 Friday

31 Saturday

September 2024

1 Sunday   14 Sunday after Trinity
Giles
Sun rises 06.18, sets 19.51

2 Monday

3 Tuesday   New Moon 01.56

4 Wednesday

5 Thursday

6 Friday

7 Saturday   *Evurtius, Bishop of Orleans*

September 2024

8 Sunday   15 Sunday after Trinity
Nativity of the BVM
Sun rises 06.29, sets 19.35
Accession of King Charles III, 2022

9 Monday   St Giles' Fair

10 Tuesday   St Giles' Fair

11 Wednesday   Moon's First Quarter 06.06

12 Thursday

13 Friday

14 Saturday   **Holy Cross Day**

September 2024

15 Sunday   16 Sunday after Trinity
Sun rises 06.40, sets 19.19

16 Monday

17 Tuesday   *Lambert*

18 Wednesday   Full Moon 02.34
Partial Eclipse of the Moon begins 02.12, ends 03.17

19 Thursday

20 Friday

21 Saturday   **St Matthew**

_____

_____

_____

_____

_____

_____

_____

September 2024

22 Sunday   17 Sunday after Trinity
Sun rises 06.52, sets 19.02
Autumnal Equinox

23 Monday

24 Tuesday   Moon's Last Quarter 18.50

25 Wednesday   Ember Day

26 Thursday   *Cyprian*

27 Friday   Ember Day

28 Saturday   Ember Day

_____

_____

_____

_____

_____

_____

_____

September/October 2024

29 Sunday   18 Sunday after Trinity
St Michael and All Angels
Quarter Day
Sun rises 07.03, sets 18.46

30 Monday   *Jerome*

1 Tuesday   *Remigius*
MICHAELMAS TERM begins
Cambridge Michaelmas Term begins

2 Wednesday   New Moon 18.49

3 Thursday   **First Day of Jewish New Year (5785)**

4 Friday   *Francis of Assisi*

5 Saturday

October 2024

6 Sunday 19 Sunday after Trinity
Faith
Sun rises 07.15, sets 18.30

7 Monday

8 Tuesday Cambridge Full Term begins

9 Wednesday *Denys*

10 Thursday Moon's First Quarter 18.55

11 Friday

12 Saturday **Yom Kippur**

October 2024

13 Sunday
20 Sunday after Trinity
Translation of King Edward, Confessor
Sun rises 07.27, sets 18.15
FULL TERM begins

14 Monday

15 Tuesday Congregation

16 Wednesday

17 Thursday
Etheldreda
First Day of Sukkot
Full Moon 11.26

18 Friday **St Luke**

19 Saturday
Frideswide
Matriculation Ceremony

October 2024

20 Sunday   21 Sunday after Trinity
Sun rises 07.39, sets 18.00

21 Monday

22 Tuesday   Congregation

23 Wednesday

24 Thursday   Moon's Last Quarter 08.03

25 Friday   *Crispin*

26 Saturday

October/November 2024

27 Sunday   22 Sunday after Trinity (or Last after Trinity)
Sun rises 06.51, sets 16.46
Summer Time ends 01.00

28 Monday   **St Simon and St Jude**

29 Tuesday

30 Wednesday

31 Thursday

1 Friday   **All Saints' Day**
New Moon 12.47

2 Saturday   *All Souls' Day*

November 2024

3 Sunday   23 Sunday after Trinity (4 before Advent)
Sun rises 07.04, sets 16.33

4 Monday

5 Tuesday   Congregation

6 Wednesday

7 Thursday

8 Friday

9 Saturday   Moon's First Quarter 05.55

November 2024

10 Sunday   24 Sunday after Trinity (3 before Advent)
Remembrance Sunday
Sun rises 07.16, sets 16.21

11 Monday

12 Tuesday

13 Wednesday

14 Thursday   King Charles III born, 1948

15 Friday   Full Moon 21.29

16 Saturday

November 2024

17 Sunday   25 Sunday after Trinity (2 before Advent)
Sun rises 07.28, sets 16.11

18 Monday

19 Tuesday   Congregation

20 Wednesday

21 Thursday

22 Friday

23 Saturday   Moon's Last Quarter 01.28

November 2024

24 Sunday   Sunday next before Advent (Christ the King)
                        Sun rises 07.40, sets 16.04

---

25 Monday

---

26 Tuesday

---

27 Wednesday

---

28 Thursday

---

29 Friday

---

30 Saturday   **St Andrew**

December 2024

1 Sunday   1 Sunday in Advent
Sun rises 07.50, sets 15.58
New Moon 06.21

2 Monday

3 Tuesday   Congregation

4 Wednesday

5 Thursday   Matriculation Ceremony

6 Friday   Cambridge Full Term ends

7 Saturday   **FULL TERM ends**

December 2024

8 Sunday   2 Sunday in Advent
Sun rises 07.59, sets 15.55
Moon's First Quarter 15.27

9 Monday

10 Tuesday

11 Wednesday   Ember Day

12 Thursday

13 Friday   Ember Day

14 Saturday   Ember Day

December 2024

15 Sunday   3 Sunday in Advent
Sun rises 08.06, sets 15.55
Full Moon 09.02

16 Monday

17 Tuesday   **MICHAELMAS TERM ends**
Congregation

18 Wednesday

19 Thursday   Cambridge Michaelmas Term ends

20 Friday

21 Saturday   **St Thomas**
Winter Solstice

December 2024

22 Sunday   4 Sunday in Advent
Sun rises 08.10, sets 15.57
Moon's Last Quarter 22.18

23 Monday

24 Tuesday

25 Wednesday   **Christmas Day**
Quarter Day
Bank Holiday

26 Thursday   **St Stephen**
Bank Holiday
First Day of Chanukah

27 Friday   **St John the Evangelist**

28 Saturday   **Innocents' Day**

_____

_____

_____

_____

_____

_____

_____

December 2024/January 2025

29 Sunday   1 Sunday after Christmas
Sun rises 08.12, sets 16.03

30 Monday   New Moon 22.27

31 Tuesday

1 Wednesday   **Circumcision (Naming of Jesus)**
Bank Holiday

2 Thursday

3 Friday

4 Saturday

DATES FOR 2025

January

February

March

April

May

June

July

August

September

October

November

December

UNIVERSITY OF OXFORD   01865 270000

University Offices, Wellington Sq, OX1 2JD
www.ox.ac.uk

University Officers

Chancellor Rt Hon Lord Patten of Barnes, KG, CH, PC, Hon Fellow Ball and St Ant

High Steward Rt Hon Lord Reed, PC, FRSE

Vice-Chancellor Prof I Tracey, FMedSci

Pro-Vice-Chancellor (*Development and External Affairs*) Prof D M Gann, CEng, FICE, FCGI

Pro-Vice-Chancellor (*Education*) Prof M Williams, New

Pro-Vice-Chancellor (*People and Digital*) Prof A E Trefethen, STX

Pro-Vice-Chancellor (*Planning and Resources*) Dr D Prout

Pro-Vice-Chancellor (*Research*) Prof P Grant, FIMMM, FREng, St Cath

Pro-Vice-Chancellor (*Innovation*) Prof C Bountra

Chief Diversity Officer Prof T Soutphommasane

Pro-Vice-Chancellors Lady Elish Angiolini, KC, FRSE, Principal of St Hugh; Prof R Goodman, FACSS, Warden of St Ant; Prof F D R Hobbs, FMedSci, FRCP, FRCGP, FRCPE, Head of Nuffield Dept of Primary Care Health Sciences; Prof J Michie, Kellogg; Prof Sir Nigel Shadbolt, FRS, FREng, FBCS, Principal of Jesus; Very Revd Prof J Shaw, Principal of Harris Man; Prof L Tarassenko, FREng, FMedSci, President of Reuben College; Prof Sir Richard Trainor, ACSS, FRHistS, Rector of Ex; Prof K J Willis, Principal of St Edmund Hall

Proctors (*2023–24*) Dr K Murphy, Oriel; Prof D Kirk, Nuffield

Proctors (*2024–25*) Prof C Mac Niocaill, Exeter; Prof T Adcock, St Peter's

Pro-Proctors (*2023–24*) Dr C Gillhammer; Dr T Franklinos; Dr D Leasure; Prof R Kashyap

Assessor (*2023–24*) Prof J Conlon, New

Assessor (*2024–25*) Prof B Bollig, St Cath

Deputy Steward Mr B J Taylor, Hon Fellow St J

Public Orator Dr J B Katz, All S

Heads of Division Prof D Grimley (*Humanities*); Prof S Howison (*Mathematical, Physical and Life Sciences*); Prof G Screaton, FMedSci, FRCP (*Medical Sciences*); Prof T Power (*Social Sciences*)

Council of the University

For the latest membership of Council please see:
https://governance.admin.ox.ac.uk/council/members-council

Divisional Boards

For the latest membership of the divisional boards please see:
www.humanities.ox.ac.uk/board-members
www.medsci.ox.ac.uk/medical-sciences-board
www.socsci.ox.ac.uk/ssdboardmembership
www.mpls.ox.ac.uk/divisional-board

University Administration and Services

For details of the University's administrative departments please see:
https://staff.admin.ox.ac.uk/structure-and-organisation/professional-services-and-university-administration#sections

ACADEMIC AND ADMINISTRATIVE INSTITUTIONS

Contact details for departments, colleges, and other affiliated parts of the collegiate University are listed alphabetically below.

ACCOMMODATION OFFICE (GRADUATE) 280923

4 Worcester Street, OX1 2BX
www.admin.ox.ac.uk/accommodation

ADMISSIONS

Graduate Admissions 270059

University Offices, Wellington Sq, OX1 2JD
www.ox.ac.uk/admissions/graduate
Director Dr N Pollini

Undergraduate Admissions and Outreach 288000

www.ox.ac.uk/study
study@ox.ac.uk
Director Dr S Khan

ALL SOULS COLLEGE 279379

High St, OX1 4AL
www.asc.ox.ac.uk
Warden Prof Sir John Vickers, FBA

ALUMNI OFFICE 611610

University Offices, Wellington Sq, OX1 2JD
www.alumni.ox.ac.uk
Director Ms C Fairchild

AMERICAN INSTITUTE, ROTHERMERE 282705

1a South Parks Rd, OX1 3UB
www.rai.ox.ac.uk
Director Prof A Smith

ANTHROPOLOGY AND MUSEUM ETHNOGRAPHY, SCHOOL 274671

51–53 Banbury Rd, OX2 6PE
www.anthro.ox.ac.uk
Head Dr D Pratten

ARBORETUM, HARCOURT 610305

Nuneham Courtenay, OX44 9PX
www.obga.ox.ac.uk
Director Prof S J Hiscock
For opening hours, ticket prices and booking please visit our website

Academic and Administrative Institutions

ARCHAEOLOGY, SCHOOL   288040

1 South Parks Road, Oxford, OX1 3TG
www.arch.ox.ac.uk
Head Prof C B Ramsey

ARCHIVES, UNIVERSITY   277145

Bodleian Library, OX1 3BG
www.bodleian.ox.ac.uk/universityarchives
Keeper Ms F McLeod

ART, RUSKIN SCHOOL   276940

74 High St, OX1 4BG
www.rsa.ox.ac.uk
Head Prof I Kiaer

ASHMOLEAN MUSEUM   278000

Beaumont St, OX1 2PH
www.ashmolean.org
Director Dr A Sturgis

Opening hours: Every day, including bank holiday Mon, 10am–5pm; Café: Every day 10am-4.30pm; Rooftop Restaurant: Mon, Tues, Wed, Sun 10am-4.30pm, Thurs–Sat 10am-10pm. Free admission except to special exhibitions

ASIAN AND MIDDLE EASTERN STUDIES,   278200
FACULTY

Pusey Lane, OX1 2LE
www.ames.ox.ac.uk
Chair of the Faculty Board Prof D Rechter

BALLIOL COLLEGE   277777

Broad St, OX1 3BJ
www.balliol.ox.ac.uk
Master Dame Helen Ghosh

BATE COLLECTION OF MUSICAL   276139
INSTRUMENTS

Faculty of Music, St Aldate's, OX1 1DB
www.bate.ox.ac.uk
Manager Mr A Lamb

Opening hours: open all year Mon–Fri 2–5pm; Sat in full term 10am–noon

BEGBROKE DIRECTORATE   283700

Begbroke Science Park, Woodstock Rd, Begbroke, OX5 1PF
www.begbroke.ox.ac.uk
Director Mr A I Cory

Academic and Administrative Institutions

BIOCHEMISTRY, DEPT   613200

South Parks Rd, OX1 3QU
www.bioch.ox.ac.uk
Head Prof F Barr

BIOLOGY, DEPT   271297

11a Mansfield Rd, OX1 3SZ
and South Parks Rd, OX1 3RB
www.biology.ox.ac.uk
Joint Heads Prof T Coulson and Prof M Fricker

BLACKFRIARS HALL   278400

St Giles', OX1 3LY
www.bfriars.ox.ac.uk
Regent Revd Dr J D O'Connor, OP

BODLEIAN LIBRARIES   277000

Broad St, OX1 3BG
www.bodleian.ox.ac.uk
Bodley's Librarian Mr R Ovenden, FRSA, FSA

Opening hours may vary and at time of printing, reading room slots must be booked in advance – please check online before visiting. Libraries (except in hospitals) are closed at least 24 Dec–1 Jan incl, Good Fri–Easter Mon incl. Many smaller libraries close for some weeks during the Long Vacation.

Alexander Library of Ornithology   272844/271143

Bodleian Book Storage Facility (BSF) in Swindon
https://libguides.bodleian.ox.ac.uk/ornithology

Bodleian Education Library   274028

15 Norham Gardens, OX2 6PY
www.bodleian.ox.ac.uk/education

Bodleian Health Care Libraries

Cairns Library   221936

Level 3, Academic Centre, JR Hospital, OX3 9DU
www.bodleian.ox.ac.uk/medicine

Horton Library   229316

Terence Mortimer Education Centre,
Horton General Hospital, OX16 9AL
www.bodleian.ox.ac.uk/medicine

Knowledge Centre site   289410

Old Rd Research Building, off Roosevelt Drive, OX3 7DQ
www.bodleian.ox.ac.uk/medicine

Academic and Administrative Institutions

Nuffield Orthopaedic Centre   **738147**

Nuffield Orthopaedic Centre, Windmill Road, OX3 7HE
www.bodleian.ox.ac.uk/medicine

Bodleian History Faculty Library   **277262**

Radcliffe Camera, OX1 3BG
www.bodleian.ox.ac.uk/history

Bodleian Japanese Library   **284506**

Nissan Institute, 27 Winchester Rd, OX2 6NA
www.bodleian.ox.ac.uk/bjl

Bodleian K B Chen China Centre Library   **280430**

Dickson Poon Building, Canterbury Road, OX2 6LU
www.bodleian.ox.ac.uk/ccl

Bodleian Latin American Centre Library   **274483**

1 Church Walk, OX2 6LY
www.bodleian.ox.ac.uk/lac

Bodleian Law Library   **271462**

St Cross Building, Manor Rd, OX1 3UR
www.bodleian.ox.ac.uk/law

Bodleian Music Faculty Library   **276148**

St Aldate's, OX1 1DB
www.bodleian.ox.ac.uk/music

Bodleian Social Science Library   **271093**

Manor Rd Building, OX1 3UQ
www.bodleian.ox.ac.uk/ssl

English Faculty Library   **271050**

St Cross Building, Manor Rd, OX1 3UQ
www.bodleian.ox.ac.uk/english

History of Medicine Library   **274604**

45–47 Banbury Rd, OX2 6PE
www.bodleian.ox.ac.uk/historyofmedicine

Leopold Muller Memorial Library (Hebrew and Jewish Studies)   **610444**

Clarendon Institute, OX1 2HG
www.bodleian.ox.ac.uk/muller

Nizami Ganjavi Library at the Faculty of Asian and Middle Eastern Studies   **278201**

Pusey Lane, OX1 2LE
www.bodleian.ox.ac.uk/nizami-ganjavi-library

Academic and Administrative Institutions

Philosophy and Theology Faculties Library   **276927**

Radcliffe Humanities, Woodstock Rd, OX2 6GG
www.bodleian.ox.ac.uk/ptfl

Radcliffe Science Library

Closed for redevelopment.
Library services temporarily moved to Vere Harmsworth Library

Rewley House Continuing Education   **270454**
Library

1 Wellington Sq, OX1 2JA
www.bodleian.ox.ac.uk/conted

Sackler Library (Archaeology, Art History   **278092**
and Classics)

1 St John St, OX1 2LG
www.bodleian.ox.ac.uk/sackler

Sainsbury Library (Saïd Business School)   **288880**

Park End St, OX1 1HP
www.bodleian.ox.ac.uk/business

Sherardian Library of Plant Taxonomy   **272844**

Dept of Biology, South Parks Rd, OX1 3RB
https://libguides.bodleian.ox.ac.uk/plant_taxonomy

Taylor Institution Library   **278158**
(Medieval and Modern Languages)

St Giles', OX1 3NA
www.bodleian.ox.ac.uk/taylor

Vere Harmsworth Library (Rothermere   **282700**
American Institute)

1a South Parks Rd, OX1 3UB
www.bodleian.ox.ac.uk/vhl

Weston Library   **277150**

Broad Street, OX1 3BG
www.bodleian.ox.ac.uk/weston

BOTANIC GARDEN, OXFORD   **610300**

Rose Lane, OX1 4AZ
www.obga.ox.ac.uk
Director Prof S J Hiscock

For opening hours, ticket prices and booking please visit our website

BRASENOSE COLLEGE   **277830**

Radcliffe Square, OX1 4AJ
www.bnc.ox.ac.uk
Principal Mr J Bowers, QC

Academic and Administrative Institutions

BUSINESS SCHOOL, SAÏD   288800

Park End St, OX1 1HP
www.sbs.ox.ac.uk
Dean Prof S Dutta

CAMPION HALL   286100

Brewer St, OX1 1QS
www.campion.ox.ac.uk
Master Revd Dr N Austin, SJ

CAREERS SERVICE   274646

56 Banbury Rd, OX2 6PA
www.careers.ox.ac.uk
Director Mr J Black

CHEMISTRY, DEPT   285000

Chemistry Research Laboratory, 12 Mansfield Rd, OX1 3TA
www.chem.ox.ac.uk
Head Prof S Faulkner

CHINA CENTRE   280387

Dickson Poon Building, Canterbury Rd, OX2 6LU
www.chinacentre.ox.ac.uk
Director Prof T Hall

CHRIST CHURCH   276150

St Aldate's, OX1 1DP
www.chch.ox.ac.uk
Dean Revd Canon Prof S Foot

CHRIST CHURCH PICTURE GALLERY   276172

Christ Church, OX1 1DP (entrance via Oriel Sq)
www.chch.ox.ac.uk/gallery
Curator Ms J Thalmann

Opening hours: Mon, Thu–Sat 11am–5pm, Sun 2–5pm (closed
Tue and Wed). Admission £6; concessions £3 (free to all members
of the University)

CLASSICS, FACULTY, AND IOANNOU CENTRE   288391
FOR CLASSICAL AND BYZANTINE STUDIES

66 St Giles', OX1 3LU
www.classics.ox.ac.uk
Chair of the Faculty Board Dr N McLynn

CLINICAL NEUROSCIENCES, NUFFIELD DEPT   234829

JR Hospital, OX3 9DU
www.ndcn.ox.ac.uk
Head Prof K Talbot FRCP

Academic and Administrative Institutions

CLUB, UNIVERSITY   271044

11 Mansfield Rd, OX1 3SZ
www.club.ox.ac.uk
Senior Facilities Manager Ms C Morgan

CLUBS OFFICE   280183

Proctors' Office, University Offices, Wellington Sq, OX1 2JD
www.ox.ac.uk/students/life/clubs

COMPAS (CENTRE ON MIGRATION, POLICY   274711
AND SOCIETY)

58 Banbury Rd, OX2 6QS
www.compas.ox.ac.uk
Director Dr C Vargas-Silva

COMPUTER SCIENCE, DEPT   273838

Wolfson Building, Parks Rd, OX1 3QD
www.cs.ox.ac.uk
Head Prof L A Goldberg

CONFERENCE OF COLLEGES   280769

University Offices, Wellington Sq, OX1 2JD
www.confcoll.ox.ac.uk
Director Ms J Finch

CONTINUING EDUCATION, DEPT   270360

1 Wellington Sq, OX1 2JA
www.conted.ox.ac.uk
Director Prof M Weait

CORPUS CHRISTI COLLEGE   276700

Merton St, OX1 4JF
www.ccc.ox.ac.uk
President Prof H Moore

DIVINITY SCHOOL   287400

Bodleian Library, Broad St, OX1 3BG
https://visit.bodleian.ox.ac.uk

Opening hours: Mon–Fri 9am–5pm, Sat 10am–5pm, Sun
11am–4pm, last ticket sold at 4.40pm. Closed on degree days and
for special events. Opening hours may vary at short notice,
so please check our website before visiting. Admission £2.50
(under-5s free). Access through Bodleian Library quadrangle

DOCTORAL TRAINING CENTRE   610988

1–4 Keble Rd, OX1 3NP
www.dtc.ox.ac.uk
Director Prof D Gavaghan

Academic and Administrative Institutions

EARTH SCIENCES, DEPT 272000

South Parks Rd, OX1 3AN
www.earth.ox.ac.uk
Head Prof M Kendall, FRS

ECONOMICS, DEPT 271089

Manor Rd Building, Manor Rd, OX1 3UQ
www.economics.ox.ac.uk
Head Prof H Low

EDUCATION, DEPT 274024

15 Norham Gardens, OX2 6PY
www.education.ox.ac.uk
Director Prof V Murphy

ENGINEERING SCIENCE, DEPT 273000

Parks Rd, OX1 3PJ
www.eng.ox.ac.uk
Head Prof R Roy

ENGLISH, FACULTY 271055

St Cross Building, Manor Rd, OX1 3UL
www.english.ox.ac.uk
Chair of the Faculty Board Prof M Turner

ENTERPRISE AND THE ENVIRONMENT, 614963
SMITH SCHOOL

South Parks Road, OX1 3QY
www.smithschool.ox.ac.uk
Director Prof C Hepburn

ERTEGUN HOUSE 615356

37a St Giles, OX1 3LD
www.ertegun.ox.ac.uk
Director Prof G Rosser

EXETER COLLEGE 279600

Turl St, OX1 3DP
www.exeter.ox.ac.uk
Rector Prof Sir Richard Trainor, ACSS, FRHistS

EXPERIMENTAL PSYCHOLOGY, DEPT 271444

Anna Watts Building, Radcliffe Observatory Quarter,
Woodstock Road, Oxford OX2 6GG
www.psy.ox.ac.uk
Head Prof M Rushworth, FRS

Academic and Administrative Institutions

GEOGRAPHY AND THE ENVIRONMENT, SCHOOL 285070

South Parks Rd, OX1 3QY
www.geog.ox.ac.uk
Head Prof G Wiggs

GOVERNMENT, BLAVATNIK SCHOOL 614343

Radcliffe Observatory Quarter, OX2 6GG
www.bsg.ox.ac.uk
Dean Prof N T Woods

GREEN TEMPLETON COLLEGE 274770

Woodstock Rd, OX2 6HG
www.gtc.ox.ac.uk
Principal Sir Michael Dixon

HARRIS MANCHESTER COLLEGE 271006

Mansfield Rd, OX1 3TD
www.hmc.ox.ac.uk
Principal Very Revd Prof J Shaw

HERTFORD COLLEGE 279400

Catte St, OX1 3BW
www.hertford.ox.ac.uk
Principal Mr T Fletcher

HISTORY, FACULTY 615000

George St, OX1 2RL
www.history.ox.ac.uk
Chair of the Faculty Board Prof R Iliffe

HISTORY OF ART DEPT AND CENTRE FOR VISUAL STUDIES (FACULTY OF HISTORY) 286830

Suite 9, Littlegate House, 16/17 St Ebbe's St, OX1 1PT
www.hoa.ox.ac.uk
Head Prof G Batchen

HISTORY OF SCIENCE MUSEUM 277293

Broad St, OX1 3AZ
www.hsm.ox.ac.uk
Director Dr S M Ackermann
Opening hours: Tues–Sun noon–5pm

HUMANITIES DIVISIONAL OFFICE 280106

Radcliffe Humanities, Radcliffe Observatory Quarter, OX2 6GG
www.humanities.ox.ac.uk
Head Prof D Grimley

Academic and Administrative Institutions

TORCH (The Oxford Research Centre in the Humanities)   280101

Radcliffe Observatory Quarter, OX2 6GG
www.torch.ox.ac.uk
Director Prof W Williams

INTERNATIONAL DEVELOPMENT, DEPT (QUEEN ELIZABETH HOUSE)   281800

3 Mansfield Rd, OX1 3TB
www.qeh.ox.ac.uk
Head Prof D Sánchez-Ancochea

INTERNET INSTITUTE, OXFORD   287210

1 St Giles', OX1 3JS
www.oii.ox.ac.uk
Director Dr V Nash

IT SERVICES   273200

13 Banbury Rd, OX2 6NN
www.it.ox.ac.uk
Chief Information Officer Dr S Duffy

Opening hours: Mon–Fri 8.30am–5.30pm. Closed approximately 10 days at Christmas, and all bank holidays. Most facilities available nights and weekends by remote access. Phone support available 24/7 on 01865 612345

JESUS COLLEGE   279700

Turl St, OX1 3DW
www.jesus.ox.ac.uk
Principal Prof Sir Nigel Shadbolt, FRS, FREng

KEBLE COLLEGE   272727

Parks Rd, OX1 3PG
www.keble.ox.ac.uk
Warden Dr Sir Michael Jacobs

KELLOGG COLLEGE   612000

Banbury Rd, OX2 6PN
www.kellogg.ox.ac.uk
President Prof J Michie

LADY MARGARET HALL   274300

Norham Gardens, OX2 6QA
www.lmh.ox.ac.uk
Principal Prof S Blyth

Academic and Administrative Institutions

NEW COLLEGE 279500

Holywell St, OX1 3BN
www.new.ox.ac.uk
Warden Mr M Young

NUFFIELD COLLEGE 278500

New Rd, OX1 1NF
www.nuffield.ox.ac.uk
Warden Sir Andrew Dilnot

ONCOLOGY, DEPT 617331

Old Rd Campus Research Building, OX3 7DQ
www.oncology.ox.ac.uk
Head Prof M R Middleton, FRCP

ORIEL COLLEGE 276555

Oriel Sq, OX1 4EW
www.oriel.ox.ac.uk
Provost Lord Mendoza of King's Reach

ORTHOPAEDICS, RHEUMATOLOGY AND 227374
MUSCULOSKELETAL SCIENCES, NUFFIELD DEPT

Nuffield Orthopaedic Centre, OX3 7HE
www.ndorms.ox.ac.uk
Head Prof J L Rees, FRCS

OXFORD MARTIN SCHOOL 287430

34 Broad St, OX1 3BD
www.oxfordmartin.ox.ac.uk
Director Prof Sir Charles Godfray

OXFORD SCHOOL OF GLOBAL AND AREA 284779
STUDIES

12 Bevington Rd, OX2 6LH
www.area-studies.ox.ac.uk
Head Prof P Chaisty

OXFORD UNIVERSITY INNOVATION LTD 280830

Buxton Court, 3 West Way, OX2 0JB
www.innovation.ox.ac.uk
CEO Dr M Perkins

PAEDIATRICS, DEPT 234240

JR Hospital, OX3 9DU
www.paediatrics.ox.ac.uk
Head Prof G A P Holländer, FMH, FRCPCH

Academic and Administrative Institutions

PARKS, UNIVERSITY — 282040

Office: Tentorium, South Lodge, South Parks Rd, OX1 3RF
www.parks.ox.ac.uk
Head of Parks/Superintendent Dr C Jenkins
Operations Manager/Deputy Head of Parks Mr P Hutchinson
Opening hours: daily 7.45am to dusk, except 24 Dec

PATHOLOGY, SIR WILLIAM DUNN SCHOOL — 275500

South Parks Rd, OX1 3RE
www.path.ox.ac.uk
Head Prof M Freeman

PEMBROKE COLLEGE — 276444

Pembroke Sq, OX1 1DW
www.pmb.ox.ac.uk
Master Rt Hon Sir Ernest Ryder, PC, KC, FRCP, FRSA

PHARMACOLOGY, DEPT — 271850

Mansfield Rd, OX1 3QT
www.pharm.ox.ac.uk
Head Prof F Platt

PHILOSOPHY, FACULTY — 276926

Radcliffe Humanities, Woodstock Rd, OX2 6GG
www.philosophy.ox.ac.uk
Chair of the Faculty Board Prof U Coope

PHYSICS, DEPT — 272200

Clarendon Laboratory, Parks Rd, OX1 3PU
www.physics.ox.ac.uk
Head Prof I Shipsey, FRS

PHYSIOLOGY, ANATOMY AND GENETICS, DEPT — 272500

Parks Rd, OX1 3PT
www.dpag.ox.ac.uk
Head Prof D J Paterson

PITT RIVERS MUSEUM — 613000

South Parks Rd, OX1 3PP
www.prm.ox.ac.uk
Director Prof L N K Van Broekhoven

Opening hours: Mon noon–5pm; Tues–Sun 10am–5pm; free admission (entry through Museum of Natural History)

POLITICS AND INTERNATIONAL RELATIONS, DEPT — 278700

Manor Rd, OX1 3UQ
www.politics.ox.ac.uk
Joint Heads Prof P Schleiter and Dr N Owen

Academic and Administrative Institutions

POPULATION AGEING, OXFORD INSTITUTE 612800

66 Banbury Rd, OX2 6PR
www.ageing.ox.ac.uk
Director Prof S Harper

POPULATION HEALTH, NUFFIELD DEPT 743743

Richard Doll Building, Old Road Campus, OX3 7LF
www.ndph.ox.ac.uk
Head Prof Sir Rory Collins, FRS, FMedSci

PRESS, OXFORD UNIVERSITY (OUP) 556767

Great Clarendon St, OX2 6DP
www.oup.com
Secretary to the Delegates and Chief Executive Mr N D Portwood

PRIMARY CARE HEALTH SCIENCES, 289300
NUFFIELD DEPT

Radcliffe Observatory Quarter, Woodstock Rd, OX2 6GG
www.phc.ox.ac.uk
Head Prof F D R Hobbs, FMedSci, FRCP, FRCGP, FRCPE

PROCTORS' OFFICE 270276

University Offices, Wellington Sq, OX1 2JD
www.proctors.ox.ac.uk
Clerk to the Proctors Mr P Mandeville

Proctors' Officers 277223

Clarendon Building, Broad St, OX1 3AZ

PSYCHIATRY, DEPT 618200

Warneford Hospital, OX3 7JX
www.psych.ox.ac.uk
Head Prof B Lennox, DM, FRCPsych

QUANTITATIVE FINANCE, OXFORD–MAN 616600
INSTITUTE

Eagle House, Walton Well Rd, OX2 6ED
www.oxford-man.ox.ac.uk
Director Prof Á Cartea

QUEEN'S COLLEGE, THE 279120

High St, OX1 4AW
www.queens.ox.ac.uk
Provost Dr C H Craig

REGENT'S PARK COLLEGE 288120

Pusey St, OX1 2LB
www.rpc.ox.ac.uk
Principal Prof Sir Malcolm Evans

Academic and Administrative Institutions

REUBEN COLLEGE   616477

1–2 South Parks Rd, Oxford OX1 3QP
www.reuben.ox.ac.uk
President Prof L Tarassenko, FREng, FMedSci

RIPON COLLEGE CUDDESDON   874404

Wheatley Rd, Cuddesdon, OX44 9EX
www.rcc.ac.uk
Principal Rt Revd H Southern

ST ANNE'S COLLEGE   274800

Woodstock Rd, OX2 6HS
www.st-annes.ox.ac.uk
Principal Ms H King

ST ANTONY'S COLLEGE   284700

Woodstock Rd, OX2 6JF
www.sant.ox.ac.uk
Warden Prof R Goodman, FACSS

ST CATHERINE'S COLLEGE   271700

Manor Rd, OX1 3UJ
www.stcatz.ox.ac.uk
Master Prof K E Börjars

ST CROSS COLLEGE   278490

St Giles', OX1 3LZ
www.stx.ox.ac.uk
Master Mrs K Mavor

ST EDMUND HALL   279000

Queen's Lane, OX1 4AR
www.seh.ox.ac.uk
Principal Prof K J Willis

ST HILDA'S COLLEGE   276884

Cowley Place, OX4 1DY
www.sthildas.ox.ac.uk
Principal Prof Dame Sarah Springman, FREng

ST HUGH'S COLLEGE   274900

St Margaret's Rd, OX2 6LE
www.st-hughs.ox.ac.uk
Principal Lady Elish Angiolini, KC, FRSE

ST JOHN'S COLLEGE   277300

St Giles', OX1 3JP
www.sjc.ox.ac.uk
President Prof Dame Sue Black, FRSE, FRAI, FRSB, ChFA

Academic and Administrative Institutions

ST PETER'S COLLEGE   278900

New Inn Hall St, OX1 2DL
www.spc.ox.ac.uk
Master Prof J Buchanan

ST STEPHEN'S HOUSE   613500

16 Marston St, OX4 1JX
www.ssho.ox.ac.uk
Principal Revd Canon Dr R Ward

SHELDONIAN THEATRE   277299

Broad St, OX1 3AZ
www.admin.ox.ac.uk/sheldonian
Chairman of the Curators Dr A Fairweather-Tall
Opening hours (subject to change): Winter time: 10am – last entry
3.30pm. BST: 10am – last entry 4pm. Closed Christmas Day,
Boxing Day, New Year's Day and when in use for ceremonies
and external events. Admission free for University members and
3 guests

SOCIAL POLICY AND INTERVENTION, DEPT   270325

Barnett House, 32 Wellington Sq, OX1 2ER
www.spi.ox.ac.uk
Head Prof J Barlow

SOCIAL SCIENCES DIVISIONAL OFFICE   614850

Hayes House, 75 George St, OX1 2BQ
www.socsci.ox.ac.uk
Head Prof T Power

SOCIOLOGY, DEPT   281740

42–43 Park End Street, Oxford, OX1 1JD
www.sociology.ox.ac.uk
Head Prof F Varese

SOMERVILLE COLLEGE   270600

Woodstock Rd, OX2 6HD
www.some.ox.ac.uk
Principal Rt Hon Baroness Royall of Blaisdon, PC

SPORT, UNIVERSITY   611476

Iffley Rd, OX4 1EQ
www.sport.ox.ac.uk
Director Mr J Roycroft

STATISTICS, DEPT   272860

24–29 St Giles', OX1 3LB
www.stats.ox.ac.uk
Head Prof C Donnelly, FRS, FMedsci

Academic and Administrative Institutions

STUDENT WELFARE AND SUPPORT SERVICES   280012

3 Worcester Street, OX1 2BX
www.ox.ac.uk/students/welfare
Director Mr R Akinsete

SURGICAL SCIENCES, NUFFIELD DEPT   617123

JR Hospital, OX3 9DU
www.nds.ox.ac.uk
Head Prof F C Hamdy, FMedSci, FRCS, FRCSEd (Urol)

TAYLOR INSTITUTION (MODERN LANGUAGES)   278142

St Giles', OX1 3NA
www.bodleian.ox.ac.uk/taylor
Taylor Librarian J Legg

THEOLOGY AND RELIGION, FACULTY   270790

Gibson Building, Radcliffe Observatory Quarter, OX2 6GG
www.theology.ox.ac.uk
Chair of the Faculty Board Prof W Wood

TRINITY COLLEGE   279900

Broad St, OX1 3BH
www.trinity.ox.ac.uk
President Dame Hilary Boulding

UNIVERSITY COLLEGE   276602

High St, OX1 4BH
www.univ.ox.ac.uk
Master Rt Hon Baroness Valerie Amos, CH, PC

VOLTAIRE FOUNDATION   284600

99 Banbury Rd, OX2 6JX
www.voltaire.ox.ac.uk
Director Prof N E Cronk

WADHAM COLLEGE   277900

Parks Rd, OX1 3PN
www.wadham.ox.ac.uk
Warden Mr R Hannigan

WOLFSON COLLEGE   274100

Linton Rd, OX2 6UD
www.wolfson.ox.ac.uk
President Sir Tim Hitchens

WOMEN'S AND REPRODUCTIVE HEALTH,   221003
NUFFIELD DEPT

JR Hospital, OX3 9DU
www.wrh.ox.ac.uk
Head Prof K Zondervan

Academic and Administrative Institutions

WORCESTER COLLEGE   **278300**

Walton St, OX1 2HB
www.worc.ox.ac.uk
Provost Mr D Isaac

WYCLIFFE HALL   **274200**

Banbury Rd, OX2 6PW
www.wycliffe.ox.ac.uk
Principal Revd Dr M F Lloyd

TIMES OF SERVICES

CHRIST CHURCH CATHEDRAL

Worship is offered in the Cathedral every day of the year and all are welcome. The normal pattern of service is:

Sundays 8am Holy Communion, 9am College Communion (term time only), 11am Choral Eucharist, 6pm Evensong

Monday to Saturday 7.10am Morning Prayer, 7.30am Holy Communion, 1pm Holy Communion (Wednesdays only), 6pm Evensong

For general enquiries or to receive information about the Cathedral, please contact the Visitors Team 286165 or cathedral@chch.ox.ac.uk. Please check online for updates: www.chch.ox.ac.uk/cathedral

MAGDALEN COLLEGE

Members of the University and the public are welcome at all chapel services during University Term.

Sundays Sung Eucharist 11am, Choral Evensong 6pm

Every day except Mondays Choral Evensong or *Tuesdays* Compline 9pm Choral Evening Prayer 6pm

Full details of services are published in the Services and Music booklet and on both the college and choir websites (www.magd.ox.ac.uk/chapel-and-choir and www.magdalencollegechoir.com)

NEW COLLEGE

The chapel is open to visitors during college visiting hours. The public are welcomed to all services, irrespective of college visiting hours. The normal pattern of services during full term includes:

Sundays Choral Evensong 5.45pm

Weekdays Choral Evensong or Eucharist 5.45pm Saturdays, Choral Evensong 6.15pm Mondays, Tuesdays, and Fridays, Choral Vespers 6.15pm Thursdays

Full details of all services can be found on the college noticeboard, in the chapel music list, and on the websites www.newcollegechoir.com and www.new.ox.ac.uk (Choir and Chapel). Please follow the links on both websites to listen to webcasts of choral services

THE UNIVERSITY CHURCH OF ST MARY THE VIRGIN

Vicar The Revd Dr W Lamb. Church Office Administrator: Sarah Ockwell, Tel. 279111. Email: admin@universitychurch.ox.ac.uk

The church and tower are open from 9.30am to 5pm (Sundays 11.30am to 5pm)

Sundays Sung Eucharist 10.30am

Weekdays Eucharist 12.15pm

For other services and events, see website (www.universitychurch.ox.ac.uk)

MERTON COLLEGE

Members of the University and public are welcome at all services.

Sundays 9am Eucharist/Morning Prayer, 5.45pm Choral Evensong/Sung Eucharist

Mondays 6pm Choral Vespers

Tuesdays, Wednesdays, and Thursdays 6.15pm Choral Evensong
Details of all services can be found on the chapel noticeboard and at
www.merton.ox.ac.uk/chapel

THE QUEEN'S COLLEGE

Members of the University and the public are welcome at all chapel
services. The normal pattern of services during full term is:
Sundays Holy Communion 9.30am, Choral Evensong 6.15pm
Monday to Friday Morning Prayer 8.45am
Wednesday and Friday Choral Evensong 6.30pm
Full details of all services can be found at www.queens.ox.ac.uk/
chapelservices

For other times of public services please see individual college
websites, which may be found through www.ox.ac.uk

UCU (University and College Union), University of Oxford

Oxford UCU Office, 16 Wellington Square, OX1 2HY
Administration Officer: Bernadette Wheeler
Tel. 288472, email: ucu@ox.ac.uk
Branch President: David Chivall

Oxford Union

Frewin Court, OX1 3JB. Tel. 241353
Email: enquiries@oxford-union.org
Bar Open: during University Term from Mon week 0: Mon to Wed 10am to
midnight; Thurs to Sat 10am to 2am; Sun noon to 10.30pm
Library: For opening times see www.oxford-union.org
Vacation: (Library and Office only) Mon to Fri 9.30am to 5pm

Oxford University Student Union

Oxford SU represents all students at the University of Oxford
4 Worcester Street, OX1 2BX. Tel. 288452
Email: enquiries@oxfordsu.ox.ac.uk
Website: www.oxfordsu.org

Oxford Preservation Trust

10 Turn Again Lane, St Ebbe's, OX1 1QL. Tel. 242918
Chairman Revd Prof W Whyte, FRHistS, FSA
Director Deborah Dance, FRICS, IHBC, RSA
Email: info@oxfordpreservation.org.uk
Website: www.oxfordpreservation.org.uk

Oxford University Royal Naval Unit

Headquarters Falklands House, Oxpens Road, OX1 1RX.
Email: navytrgbrnc-urnuoxford@mod.gov.uk
Commanding Officer P Crease
Coxswain CPO T Pring

Oxford University Officers' Training Corps

Headquarters Falklands House, Oxpens Road, OX1 1RX. Tel. 255341
Email: RMAS-Gp-OTC-Oxford-GroupMailbox@mod.gov.uk
Commanding Officer Lt Col B Walters, RRF
Adjutant Capt E Hatzis, RA
Administrative Officer Capt I P Felstead, MBE, PWRR

Oxford University Air Squadron

Training Headquarters and Mess Falklands House, Oxpens Road, OX1 1RX
Admin Headquarters/Airfield RAF Benson, Wallingford, Oxon OX10 6AA
email: 6fts-OUAS-Admin@mod.gov.uk
Commanding Officer Squadron Leader C Aston

City of Oxford

Members of Parliament Layla Moran (Oxford West and Abingdon);
Anneliese Dodds (Oxford East)
Chief Executive Caroline Green
THE CITY COUNCIL
The City Council comprises forty-eight members
Lord Mayor Cllr James Fry

Oxfordshire County Council

The County Council comprises 63 elected councillors.
Chair Cllr Susanna Pressel
Leader Cllr Liz Leffman
County Hall, New Rd, Oxford, OX1 1ND
Website: www.oxfordshire.gov.uk/council

Oxford Civic Society

'For those keen to understand and help Oxford.'
Chairman Ian Green 723289
Hon Secretary Vernon Porter 557660
Email: info@oxcivicsoc.org.uk
Website: www.oxcivicsoc.org.uk

Royal Mail Group plc

www.royalmailgroup.com is a portal combining information and
services from Royal Mail and Parcelforce Worldwide.
Local collections For details please contact your nearest Post Office
(www.postoffice.co.uk).

AIRPORTS

Birmingham, Tel. 0871 222 0072. www.birminghamairport.co.uk
Gatwick, Tel. 0344 892 0322. www.gatwickairport.com
Heathrow, Tel. 0844 335 1801. www.heathrow.com
London City Airport, Tel. 020 7646 0088. www.londoncityairport.com
Luton, Tel. 01582 405100. www.london-luton.co.uk
Manchester, Tel. 0808 169 7030. www.manchesterairport.co.uk
Stansted, Tel. 0844 335 1803. www.stanstedairport.com

TRAINS

A timetable information service is available at www.nationalrail.co.uk

LONDON, HEATHROW, AND GATWICK COACHES

This information is subject to alteration; passengers should check before travel

Oxford Bus Company times and fares. Tel. 01865 785400
www.oxfordbus.co.uk

Oxford–Heathrow: Daily 24-hour express service between Oxford (Gloucester Green) and Heathrow. Journey time about 80 mins to Terminal 5; about 90 mins to Central Bus Station.

Oxford–Gatwick: Daily 24-hour express service between Oxford (Gloucester Green) and Gatwick. Journey time about 120–150 minutes.

Oxford–Birmingham Airport: Daily service between Oxford (Gloucester Green) and Birmingham Airport. Journey time about 120 minutes.

Oxford Tube. Tel. 01865 772250
www.oxfordtube.com

Daily 24-hour express coach service from Oxford (Gloucester Green) via Hillingdon Station to London (Shepherds Bush, Notting Hill Gate, Marble Arch, Grosvenor Gardens). Journey time about 100 minutes.

CAMBRIDGE COACHES

Coaches operate from Gloucester Green in Oxford and Drummer Street in Cambridge

National Express: Tel. 08717 818181 (all enquiries)
www.nationalexpress.com

National Express Airport (via Stansted): details as above

Stagecoach Express X5 Traveline: Tel. 0871 200 2233
www.stagecoachx5.com

Telephone Numbers

TELEPHONE NUMBERS

Code for Oxford +44 (0)1865

General emergencies 999
Police (Thames Valley non-emergency number) 101
NHS (urgent medical help or advice) 111

University Security Services 272944 (Emergencies 289999)

Main Oxford switchboard 270000
Main Cambridge switchboard 01223 337733

NOTES

The hours of sunrise and sunset for Oxford are given in Greenwich Mean Time. For the period of Summer Time one hour has been added. The phases of the moon are given in Greenwich Mean Time. They are reproduced, with permission, from data supplied by H. M. Nautical Almanac Office © Council for the Central Laboratory of the Research Councils.

Lighting-up time for vehicles is defined as being from half an hour after sunset to half an hour before sunrise throughout the year. Sidelights must be used from sunset to sunrise.

All information in this diary is as far as possible correct at the time of going to press.

Typeset by Graphicraft Ltd., Hong Kong
Printed in Great Britain by Charles Letts & Co Ltd.

National Rail
Britain's train companies working together

- Principal routes and stations
- Other main routes and stations
✈ Airport interchange
⚓ Ferry service

LONDON TERMINAL STATIONS
CC Charing Cross
EU Euston
FS Fenchurch Street
KX King's Cross
LS Liverpool Street
LB London Bridge
MA Marylebone
PA Paddington
SP St. Pancras International
VC Victoria
WA Waterloo

National Rail Enquiries
Website
www.nationalrail.co.uk
Contact Centre
03457 48 49 50

© ATOC 2015. All rights reserved. Reg. user No. 22/5/5192/P Version 8 ATOC 10.35

Telephone
Information
Services

National Rail Enquiries (24 h)	0345 7 48 49 50
Eurostar Enquiries (Passengers)	03432 186 186
Traveline	0871 200 22 33
Transport for London (24 h)	0343 222 1234

MAYOR OF LONDON

© Transport for London

Reg. user No. 23/5/3653/P

tfl.gov.uk

24 hour travel information
0343 222 1234*

Check y
tfl.go

Improvement works may affect your je